T0011168

THE WORST FAILS IN SPORTS

by Thomas Kingsley Troupe

CAPSTONE PRESS
a capstone imprint

Published by Capstone Press, an imprint of Capstone
1710 Roe Crest Drive, North Mankato, Minnesota 56003
capstonepub.com

SPORTS ILLUSTRATED KIDS is a trademark of ABG-SI LLC.
Used with permission.

Library of Congress Cataloging-in-Publication Data
Names: Troupe, Thomas Kingsley, author.
Title: Dropping the ball : the worst fails in sports / by Thomas Kingsley Troupe.
Description: North Mankato, Minnesota : Capstone Press, [2023] | Series: Sports illustrated kids. Heroes and heartbreakers | Includes bibliographical references and index. | Audience: Ages 8-11 | Audience: Grades 4-6 | Summary: "Game-ending errors, on-the-court meltdowns, and more! In this Sports Illustrated Kids book, discover the all-time worst fails in sports history. Karl Malone's missed free throws in the 1997 NBA Finals against the Chicago Bulls. Catcher Hank Gowdy of the New York Giants' tripping on his own mask and dropping the ball in 1924. Pete Sampras smashing the ball out of bounds and losing Wimbledon to George Bastl. Read about game-ending errors, on-the-court meltdowns, and more in this epic book of fails. Missing this book-jam-packed with eye-popping photos and heart-pounding text-would be an epic failure for any sports fan"— Provided by publisher.
Identifiers: LCCN 2022029349 (print) | LCCN 2022029350 (ebook) | ISBN 9781669011224 (hardcover) | ISBN 9781669011170 (paperback) | ISBN 9781669011187 (pdf) | ISBN 9781669011200 (kindle edition)
Subjects: LCSH: Sports—History—Juvenile literature. | Failure (Psychology)—Juvenile literature.
Classification: LCC GV706.4 .T755 2023 (print) | LCC GV706.4 (ebook) | DDC 796—dc23/eng/20220721
LC record available at https://lccn.loc.gov/2022029349
LC ebook record available at https://lccn.loc.gov/2022029350

Editorial Credits
Editor: Christianne Jones; Designer: Elyse White;
Media Researcher: Donna Metcalf; Production Specialist: Polly Fisher

Image and Design Element Credits
Alamy: Cal Sport Media, 12, 13, Historic Collection, 19, PA Images, 23, 26, 27, Xinhua, 21, Yogi Black, 10; Associated Press: Chris O'Meara, 25; Getty Images: Chuck Solomon, 17, Graig Abel, 9, Image Source, 28, Jed Jacobsohn, 15, Jupiterimages, 5, Koji Aoki / Aflo, cover (bottom), Noam Galai/noamgalai.com, 4, Patrik Giardino, 29; Shutterstock: afaf.asf, design element (water icon) , Iconic Bestiary, design element (golf icon), kuroksta, design element (soccer icon), Palsur, design element (sport icon); Sports Illustrated: Robert Beck, 7 (all), Simon Bruty, 16

All internet sites appearing in back matter were available and accurate when this book was sent to press.

TABLE OF CONTENTS

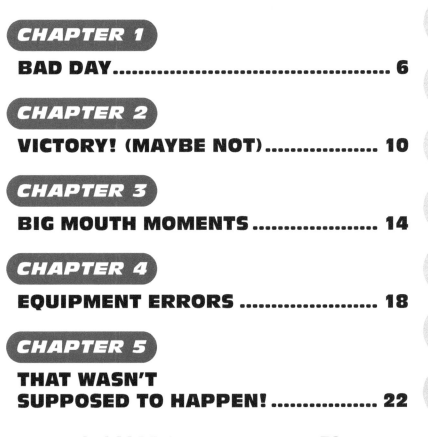

Words in **bold** are in the glossary.

NO EASY VICTORY

It should have been an easy victory. Your basketball team is rated number one. The whole world had no doubt you and your teammates would come out on top. But something happened in the first quarter, and everything began to fall apart.

You watch the opposing team drive the ball down the court for an easy dunk. They tied the game. In a matter of minutes, your team's big lead is gone.

Since sports began, players and teams have discovered there is no such thing as a sure thing. One mistake can change the course of a game. Even the greatest athletes have bad days. Take a time-out and relive some big fails in sports history.

CHAPTER 1
BAD DAY

Everyone has bad days. But not everyone has bad days in front of the whole world. Unfortunately, that is exactly what happened to some athletes during big moments.

THE FINAL NINE

Someone once said, "Golf is a good walk spoiled." During the 2011 Masters, Rory McIlroy would probably agree. That year, the 21-year-old hoped to become the second-youngest player ever to win the tournament. After the first three rounds, he was in the lead. It looked like his dream would come true.

FUN FACT

On April 13, 1997, Tiger Woods became the youngest golfer to win the Masters Tournament. He won by a record-breaking 12 strokes!

Rory McIlroy struggling at the Masters.

Everything changed nine holes into the final round. A drive hit a tree. It landed far off the fairway. McIlroy hit another tree in his attempt to find the green.

The 11th and 12th holes weren't much kinder. With a bogey and a double bogey, McIlroy's lead was gone. A drive off the 13th tee box whistled into a creek. By the end of the tournament, he was tied for 15th place.

AN UNHAPPY BIRTHDAY

Hockey is a tough sport. During the Stanley Cup playoffs on April 30, 1986, Edmonton Oilers defenseman Steve Smith had a tough day.

The Oilers were tied with the Calgary Flames 2–2 in the third period. Smith brought the puck around his net to launch it out of the defensive zone. The puck didn't go where Smith wanted. It banked off goalie Grant Fuhr's skate and bounced back into the net.

Smith had scored one for the Flames on his own goal. The Oilers never caught up and lost a chance at a third consecutive Stanley Cup. Even worse? It was Smith's 23rd birthday.

Smith skates behind the net during the 1986 playoffs.

CHAPTER 2
VICTORY!
(MAYBE NOT)

A game isn't over until it's truly over. In fact, a game can actually be done and *still* not be over!

SECOND BASE MISS

During a late-season baseball game against the Chicago Cubs in 1908, the game was tied 1–1 in the bottom of the ninth.

Merkle making his way around the bases after a home run.

New York Giants Fred Merkle was on first, and Moose McCormick was on third. Al Bridwell hit a single. McCormick ran for home.

When McCormick crossed the plate, everyone thought the Giants had won. But Merkle never touched second base. Cubs second baseman Johnny Evers was thrown the ball and touched second base. But by then the crowd had stormed the field.

The umpires met after the game to talk about the play. However, they didn't reach an agreement until the next day. Then they announced it was a tie. The game would be replayed. The Cubs won the National League pennant. Chicago went on to win the 1908 World Series against the Detroit Tigers.

A TOUGH REPUTATION

Fred Merkle never lived down his big error in the 1908 game. People were always watching for his next big mistake. In 1912, he—along with the catcher and pitcher—missed a foul pop-up that cost the Giants the World Series. A newspaper headline read, "Bonehead Merkle Does It Again."

DELAYED PENALTIES

At the 2017 ANA Inspiration women's golf tournament, Lexi Thompson had a two-stroke lead going into the final round. But when she arrived at the course, she received some terrible news. She was starting off the day with a four-stroke penalty.

Thompson on the 18th hole during the final round of play.

A TV viewer noticed that Thompson didn't put her ball back where it had been marked on the 17th green the day before. She placed it less than an inch closer to the hole. The viewer sent an email about the violation to the LPGA fan website. The judges agreed. To make matters worse, Thompson also signed the wrong scorecard for the third round. Each penalty cost her two strokes. Her lead was gone.

Despite playing an impressive final round, Thompson ended up losing the championship to So Yeon Ryu.

CHAPTER 3

BIG MOUTH MOMENTS

Sometimes it's hard to keep your mouth shut, even if you are a famous athlete. But we all know words really can hurt.

NO DELIVERIES

Sunday, June 1, 1997, was Game 1 of the NBA Finals. The Utah Jazz were pitted against the Chicago Bulls. With the game tied 82–82, the pressure was on. With 9.2 seconds left in the game, Jazz forward Karl "The Mailman" Malone was fouled. He'd get two free throws.

FUN FACT

Karl Malone got the nickname "The Mailman" because he always "delivered in the post."

Pippen (right) chatting with Malone during a playoff game.

Before Malone went to the line, Bulls forward Scottie Pippen walked up to him. "The Mailman doesn't deliver on Sunday," Pippen taunted.

Malone took his first shot. It bounced off the rim. He missed his second shot too. The Bulls got the ball and called a time-out. With seconds left on the clock, Michael Jordan made a perfect jump shot at the buzzer, winning the game 84–82.

FOOT FAULTS

Kim Clijsters came back to tennis after taking two years off to raise her first child. A few weeks later, she went head-to-head with tennis legend Serena Williams at the 2009 U.S. Open semifinal round.

Williams was frustrated after receiving a warning for breaking her racket earlier in the match. At match point in the second set, Williams served. She was called for a foot fault. She served again and foot faulted once more.

Williams yelling at a line judge during the semifinal round.

Williams was angry and yelled at the line judge. The line judge reported what she said to the officials. The match was over. Unranked Kim Clijsters went on to win the U.S. Open.

CHAPTER 4
EQUIPMENT ERRORS

Equipment is meant to help athletes stay safe and play their best. But sometimes the equipment designed to help gets in the way.

MISPLACED MASK

During the seventh and final game of the 1924 World Series, catcher Hank Gowdy of the New York Giants had equipment issues. The Giants were playing the Washington Senators. The game was tied 3–3 going into the bottom of the 12th.

Muddy Ruel stepped up to bat with one out. He swung and popped up the ball near home plate. Hoping for an easy catch, Gowdy ripped off his mask. However, he didn't throw it far enough aside. His foot got caught in the mask, and the ball dropped. Ruel's next hit was a double.

Hank Gowdy (left), Lefty Tyler (center), and Joe Connolly

After that, the Senators rallied thanks to errors. The next hit made it through the infield. With runners on first and second base, the Giants were in trouble. Then Earl McNeely hit a ground ball down the third-base line. Ruel ran home and scored the winning run in the World Series.

UNHELPFUL GOGGLES

Seventeen-year-old U.S. swimmer Lydia Jacoby was about to be part of Olympic Games history. In 2021, the Olympics introduced the 4x100-meter mixed medley relay. The event featured men and women swimming together in a relay race.

But when Jacoby dove into the pool, her goggles slipped down her face. They slid over her nose and mouth. They stayed there the entire race, making it tricky for Jacoby to see the wall. She had to swim her length with her eyes open.

Though the goggle malfunction slowed her down, Jacoby still swam an impressive race. Unfortunately, the U.S. team ended up finishing fifth.

Jacoby's goggles slipped over her mouth as she swam.

CHAPTER 5

THAT WASN'T SUPPOSED TO HAPPEN!

Sometimes the unthinkable happens. It just does. You can't explain it, and you can't change it. When it happens during a big sporting event, it's devastating and unforgettable.

ABOVE AND BEYOND

In 1994, Italy faced Brazil for the FIFA World Cup. The soccer teams battled for both periods without either team scoring. That forced the game into two periods of extra time.

FUN FACT

The 1994 World Cup Final was the first match to not have any goals scored in regular or extra time.

No goals were scored in either overtime period. The only way to determine the winner was a shootout. Each team had five different players kick penalty shots on the goal. Before long, Brazil was leading 3–2.

Roberto Baggio was asked to kick and save Italy. He is one of the greatest soccer players of all time. Baggio ran up on the ball and kicked it. The ball sailed high—too high. It flew way above the goal. Brazil was declared the winner.

Baggio walks away as Brazil celebrates their win.

WIDE RIGHT

Super Bowl XXV took place on January 27, 1991. The New York Giants and the Buffalo Bills were set to battle it out. And it was a battle!

In the fourth quarter with only seconds left on the clock, the Giants were leading 20-19. The Bills were set up for a field goal from 47 yards out. Place-kicker Scott Norwood was set to put the ball through the uprights and win the game. At first, the kick looked good. Then the ball veered wide right and missed completely. In an instant, the Bills had lost.

CAREER DEFINING

Unfortunately, a big fail on the field can define a player's entire career. Scott Norwood wasn't a bad kicker. *The Buffalo News* interviewed him the day before the big game. The headline read, "Norwood Is Ready to Win It All in Last Second." Sadly, the exact opposite happened.

Norwood walks off the field after his big miss.

THE MIGHTY FALL

In 2002 at the second round at Wimbledon, seven-time champion Pete Sampras faced George Bastl. Bastl was ranked #145 on the tennis circuit. From anyone looking at the matchup, it was clear Sampras would crush Bastl.

Sampras lunges for a ball during the match.

Bastl won the first two sets of the match. When Sampras came back and won the next two, everyone figured Sampras would win the last set and wrap it up.

In a fairy-tale ending that shocked the tennis world, Bastl came back hard. He fought a close battle in the last set. At game point, Bastl served. He and Sampras volleyed. As Bastl moved toward the net, Sampras smashed the ball too hard. It was called out. Bastl was the winner.

BACK TO THE BEGINNING

Back on the court, things just don't feel right. You throw a pass, but a rival player steals it. Your teammates keep missing free throws. Before long, the game is over. Your team stings from the epic fail.

Games and matches don't always go the way athletes or even fans think they will. There's always a chance that something will go wrong. It can completely change the direction of a game. Fails on the court and field are part of life in the competitive world of sports. Though it's never easy to accept mistakes, great fails definitely keep sports interesting!

GLOSSARY

circuit
(SUHR-kuht)
a series of races that
leads to a single
championship

consecutive
(kuhn-SEK-yuh-tiv)
when something
happens several times in
a row without a break

malfunction
(mal-FUHNGK-shun)
a failure to work
correctly

penalty
(PEN-uhl-tee)
a punishment for
breaking the rules

rally (RAL-ee)
to come from behind
to tie or take the lead

reputation
(rep-yuh-TAY-shuhn)
a person's character as
judged by other people

taunt (TAWNT)
to use words to try to
make someone angry

READ MORE

Campbell, Grace. *Great Sports Fails*. Minneapolis: Lerner Publications, 2020.

Graves, Will. *Greatest Teams That Didn't Win It All*. Minneapolis: Abdo Publishing, 2018.

Marthaler, Jon. *Bad Days In Sports*. North Mankato, MN: Capstone Press, 2017.

INTERNET SITES

Rookie Road: List of Kids Sports
rookieroad.com/sports/kids-sports-list

Sports Illustrated Kids: Greatest Upsets in Sports History
sikids.com/si-kids/greatest-upsets-sports-history

Time for Kids: Sports
timeforkids.com/g56/topics/sports

INDEX

ABOUT THE AUTHOR

Thomas Kingsley Troupe is the author of a big ol' pile of books for kids. He's written about everything from ghosts to Bigfoot to third-grade werewolves. He even wrote a book about dirt. When he's not writing or reading, he investigates the strange and spooky as part of the Twin Cities Paranormal Society. Thomas lives in Woodbury, Minnesota, with his two sons.